AF364979

Rita Oakford

Auntie Rita's

Art of German Baking

Collected recipes of Cakes & Cookies from over 40 Years

Imprint

Copyright © 2023 by Rita Oakford
Translation: Rita & Howerd Oakford

First printed in 2023

ISBN 978-3-910662-00-1

Contents

Foreword

Growing up in a community-based surrounding where my parents where the caretakers of a community house in Wolfsburg, Germany I had more fun helping in the kitchen than playing with dolls. So, I often ended up helping my Mother and Grandmother in the kitchen.

Later I got more and more into baking. At the age of 16 I started an apprentice as a pastry cook. Later I took contracts on Cruise ships (Royal Viking Star 1987/88 and Queen Elizabeth II in 1988) and in 5-star Hotels around Europe.

As a trained pastry chef, I started collecting recipes at an early stage. Over the years there were more and more recipes which ended up in a thick folder. Now, there are over three hundred recipes.

So, the desire grew in me to put them into a book and pass them on to my children. What could be better than holding a beautifully designed book in your hands?

This book is dedicated to my children and their families. I hope they enjoy the collection of recipes as much as I enjoyed writing and putting this book together.

Pastries

Pastries are baked goods made from doughs and mixtures, that can be baked on the cooker or in the oven.

Bakers and confectioners refer to these pastries as fine pastries in contrast to the so-called small pastries made of bread dough (rolls and pretzels).

In Austria, "pastry" usually refers to small baked goods (also for individual pieces).

In Germany, pastry in the narrower sense often refers to sweet baked goods such as biscuits, cakes, Danish pastry, and the like.

Here is a selection of my favourite pastries.

Kirchweihnudeln / Knieküchle

Knieküchle, also Kirchweihnudeln, Kiachl or Auszogne (Bavarian, in High German Ausgezogene), are the traditional pastries of Southern German, Austrian and South Tyrolean cuisine. They are lard-based pastries, found over a wide area, especially in Bavarian Swabia, Old Bavaria, Franconia, Austria, South Tyrol and Thuringia.

Knieküchle bear their name because it is said that the Franconian bakers drew out the dough over the knee so that it is so thin in the middle that you can read a love letter through it. Hence the saying: "Willst schäine Schissalasköichla baggn, brachst braade Gnöi" (If you want to bake beautiful Schüssel-Küchle, you need wide knees). Other names are Schüssalasküchle and, alluding slightly ironically to the wide knees, katholische Küchle.

Working time approx.30 minutes **Resting time** 45 min. -2 hrs.
Deep fryer temperature 175° C

Ingredients for approx. 12 pieces

500 g	Flour
40 g	Yeast
1/8 L	Milk
120 g	Butter
2	Egg yolks
3	Eggs
60 g	Sugar
100 ml	Cream
50 ml	Rum
50 g	Raisins (you can also omit)
	pinch of salt

Preparation

Soak the raisins in rum for at least 2 hours.
In the meantime, dissolve crumbled yeast and 1 teaspoon sugar in the lukewarm milk. Sift the flour into a large bowl, make a well in the centre, and pour in the yeast milk. Stir in a little of the flour to make a thick paste in the well. This is the so-called pre-dough,

which you now leave to rise for about 20 minutes, covered, in a warm place.

Cream the butter and sugar with the whisks of a hand mixer. Add the eggs, egg yolks, grated lemon zest, salt and rum and continue mixing until the sugar has dissolved (no longer crunches).

Pour the foamy mixture on top of the pre-dough and mix it all together with the flour (using the dough hook of a hand mixer or wooden spoon), adding enough of the lukewarm cream to make a smooth dough that pulls away from the side of the bowl. The dough must be beaten very well until it shines and bubbles. This takes a bit of time and energy but is important for the later loose consistency of the dough. Finally, add the raisins that have been squeezed out. Cover and let rise in a warm place until the dough has doubled in volume (at least 45 minutes, at room temperature possibly several hours, then the dough becomes more porous).

Form doughnuts from the dough, i.e., balls of dough with a diameter of 6 - 8 cm. There should be about 12 doughnuts. Cover again and let rise on a floured board or tray for about 30 minutes.

In the meantime, heat 1.5 kg of oil in a wide saucepan. The temperature is reached when bubbles rise on the wooden handle of a wooden spoon when dipped in the oil.

Fry the doughnuts one by one, floating in the hot oil, turning once when they are light brown. The oil should not be so hot so that the noodles get too brown on the outside and remain doughy on the inside. But it should also be hot enough, otherwise the dough will soak up fat and you won't get a fluffy pastry. You have to try it out and see.

Do not put too many doughnuts into the fat at once (no more than 4 - 5), otherwise the oil will foam or cool too much.

Place on a wire rack or on paper towels to drain. Dust the finished pasta with icing sugar and eat soon. They are especially good warm. You can reheat them in the oven the next day.

Dampfnudeln

Dampfnudel (steam-noodle, Alsatian: Dampfnüdel) is a sort of
white bread roll or sweet roll eaten as a meal or as a dessert
in Germany, Austria and in France (Alsace). It is a typical dish in
southern Germany.
The origin of the Dampfnudel is unknown. Lovers of Bavarian
cuisine as well as Palatinate cuisine therefore claim that it comes
from their respective regions.

Oven temperature 160° C convection **baking time** approx.30
minutes **Working time** approx. 30 minutes **Resting time** approx. 45
minutes

Ingredients for 9 servings

1 pinch	Salt
1	Egg
500 g	Flour, type 501
21 g	Yeast
250 ml	Milk
75 g	Sugar
½	Lemon, organic, peel thereof
50 g	Butter
1 TBSP.	Butter for the mould

Ingredients for the glaze

50 g	Butter
250 ml	Milk
50 g	Sugar

Preparation

For the steamed noodles, place the flour in a bowl. Crumble the
yeast with your hands and add to the bowl along with the egg and
lemon zest.

Put the milk in a saucepan, add the sugar, salt and butter and heat
gently.

Then add the milk-butter mixture to the flour in the bowl and work with a hand mixer, using dough hooks, until the dough is smooth and supple. If necessary, knead the dough again by hand.

Now make the yeast dough into a ball, cover with a kitchen towel and leave to rise in a warm place for about 30-45 minutes.
Once the yeast dough has reached about twice its volume, it is now time to form the "Buchteln". Form a roll from the dough, divide into 9 pieces and form small balls.
Then grease a high baking dish with a little butter and place the steamed noodle in it. The steamed noodle may be placed next to each other or with some distance in the form. It is best to place one ball in the middle and the rest of the steamed noodle around the outside.
Preheat the oven to 160 degrees, with convection heating.
Now carefully heat the milk with the butter and sugar in a saucepan and pour over the steamed noodles.
Bake the steamed noodle in the preheated oven on the lowest rack for about 25-30 minutes until golden brown.
The steamed noodles taste great when still warm, with homemade vanilla sauce, some poppy seeds or stewed apples or plums.

Franzbrötchen (Cinnamon roll)

A Franzbrötchen is a small, sweet pastry baked with butter and cinnamon, similar to a cinnamon roll. Sometimes other ingredients are used as well, such as chocolate or raisins. It is a type of pastry commonly found in Northern Germany, especially Hamburg, and it is usually served for breakfast, but is also enjoyed along with coffee and cake. As its name indicates, the Franzbrötchen was probably inspired by French pastries. Originally, it could be found only in the region of Hamburg, but now Franzbrötchen are also sold in Cologne, Berlin, and other German cities.

Working time 30 - 45 minutes **Resting time** approx. 40 minutes
Oven temperature 180° C **Baking time** approx. 25 minutes

Ingredients for 20 pieces

500 g	Flour
40 g	Yeast
70 g	Sugar
250 ml	Milk, lukewarm
70 g	Butter
1 pinch	Salt
1	Lemon untreated, zest grated

For the filling:

200 g	Butter
200 g	Sugar
2 TSP.	Cinnamon

Preparation

Put the flour in a bowl make a well in the middle. Sprinkle a little sugar, pour the milk into the well, then crumble and dissolve the yeast into the milk. Spread softened butter, the remaining sugar, salt and lemon zest over the top of the flour. Starting from the center, knead all the ingredients with your hands or a dough hook until you have a smooth dough. Cover and let rise in a warm place until doubled in volume, about 30-40 min.
Knead the dough again vigorously

Roll out a rectangle of 30x25 cm on a floured work surface.
Cut the well chilled butter into thin slices and place on one half of
the dough. Fold the other half over it. Press the edges of the dough
together and push them under the dough piece.
On the floured work surface, roll out to a rectangle of 30 x 50 cm.
From the narrow side, fold 1/3 of the dough sheet in towards the
middle and fold the last third over so that there are three layers of
dough on top of each other. Chill for 15 min.
Then roll out the dough to a size of 80 x 40 cm on the floured work
surface. Brush with water. Mix the cinnamon and sugar, and
sprinkle evenly over the dough. Roll up the dough from the long
side into a 6 cm wide flattened roll. The seam should be at the
bottom. Cut the dough roll into 4 cm wide pieces. Using a wooden
spoon handle, firmly press each piece in parallel to the cut surfaces.
Place at least 4 cm apart on 2 greased baking sheets and cover.
Let the French rolls rise for 15 - 20 min. in a warm place on the
tray that will be baked first; refrigerate the 2nd tray so that the
dough rises more slowly. Bake in a preheated oven on the middle
shelf at 200 °C top/bottom heat for approx. 15 - 25 min. (Every oven
bakes differently, so please adjust based on your own experience).

Waffles

The oldest evidence of waffle irons dates back to the 9th century and was found in Belgium and France. It is assumed that the production of wafers in the monasteries was a precursor to waffle baking.

In France, there was already a separate guild of waffle bakers in the 13th century. Hollow waffles were known by the 15th century at the latest. At that time, waffles were widespread in the Netherlands, as well as in northern Germany, the Fläming region, Brandenburg and the Baden area.

Bergische waffles (heart-shaped waffles) are a regional specialty in the Bergisches Land. The waffle baking tradition in Westphalia can be traced back to the 16th century.

In **Saarland** and the **Palatinate**, cinnamon waffles are popular traditionally at Christmas time.

They are made there both commercially and at home.

In **Belgium**, there are many small shops or stalls where fresh Brussels or Liège waffles are baked. The latter consist of a yeast dough with granulated sugar.

In the **Netherlands**, thin waffle pairs (stroopwafels) filled with syrup or honey are very common.

In **Sweden**, waffles are traditionally baked in the shape of a heart. 25 March is the official Waffle Day (Våffeldagen in Swedish).

In **Norway**, two special waffle pastries are part of the Christmas Eve tradition: Goro and Hohlhippen, which are called Krumkake there. There are special waffle irons for both. But waffles also play a very important role in Norwegian everyday life as a classic pastry with coffee. Waffles are usually served with typical Norwegian brown cheese or sour cream and strawberry jam.

Ingredients for approx. 16 pieces

300 g	Flour
1 TSP.	Baking powder
1 pinch	Salt
300 g	Butter
80 g	Sugar
6 pcs	Eggs
30 ml	Rum
1 TSP.	grated lemon peel
10 g	Vanilla sugar

Preparation

For the waffle batter, beat butter, sugar, grated lemon zest and vanilla sugar until fluffy.
Add the eggs little by little. Finally, add the rum. Sift flour and baking powder, stir in carefully.

Heat the waffle iron and pour in about 2 tablespoons of batter and bake until golden brown.

Buttermilk Waffles

Ingredients for approx. 15 pieces

250 g	Butter
100 g	Sugar
60 g	Vanilla sugar
8	Eggs
500 g	Flour
6 g	Baking powder
350 ml	Buttermilk

Preparation

For the waffle batter, beat the butter, sugar and vanilla sugar until fluffy. Add the eggs little by little.
Sift the flour and baking powder, stir in carefully.
Stir in the buttermilk carefully at the end.

Heat the waffle iron and pour in about 2 tablespoons of batter and bake until golden brown.

Baked cakes

A wide selection of delicious cakes....

From A like Apple strudel to Z like Zwetschgen (Plum) cake.
I hope you will have fun baking and also feasting....

American brownies

One legend about the creation of brownies is that of Bertha Palmer, a prominent Chicago socialite whose husband owned the Palmer House Hotel. In 1893, Palmer asked a pastry chef for a dessert suitable for ladies attending the Chicago World's Columbian Exposition. She requested a cake-like confection smaller than a piece of cake that could be included in boxed lunches. The result was the Palmer House Brownie with walnuts and an apricot glaze. Today the Palmer House Hotel serves a dessert using the same recipe. The name was given to the dessert sometime after 1893 but was not used in cookery books or journals at the time.

The first-known recipe was published in *Machias Cookbook* in 1899. They were called "Brownie's Food". The recipe appears on page 23 in the cake section of the book. Marie Kelley from Whitewater, Wisconsin, created the recipe.

The earliest-known published recipes for a modern style chocolate brownie appeared in the *Home Cookery* (1904, Laconia, NH), *Service Club Cookbook* (1904, Chicago, IL), *The Boston Globe* (April 2, 1905, p. 34), and the 1906 edition of *Fannie Farmer's* cookbook. These recipes produced a relatively mild and cake-like brownie.

Oven Temperature 180° C **Baking time** 20-25 minutes

Ingredients for approx. 24 pieces

200 g	Flour
½ TSP	Salt
230 g	Butter, in pieces
400 g	Sugar
65 ml	Espresso
300 g	Chocolate, plain
70 g	Cocoa powder, unsweetened
1 pct.	Vanilla sugar
270 ml	Eggs
250 g	Walnuts, coarsely chopped

Preparation

Preheat oven to 180 degrees. Grease rectangular form (size approx. 20 x 30 cm).
Bring butter, sugar, vanilla sugar and coffee to the boil in a saucepan over a medium heat, stirring constantly. Remove from heat. Add chocolate and stir until all chocolate is melted. Allow this chocolate mixture to cool a bit. Stir occasionally.
Fold the eggs into the mixture with a spoon and mix well.
Fold in flour and salt until everything is very well mixed and smooth. Fold in walnuts at the end.
Prepare the pan, pour the batter into it, and smooth the batter.
Bake for about 20-25 minutes. When testing with chopsticks, the dough may still stick to the lower third.
Leave to cool in the mould. Spread with glaze or ganache and allow to set. Also tastes good without glaze ....
Finally, cut into small rectangles.

Chocolate Ganache Glaze

Ingredients
180 g	Butter
375 g	Chocolate 75 %
3 tbsp	Unsweetened cocoa powder
45 ml	Coconut milk
180 g	Honey

Preparation
Melt the butter in a small saucepan over a low heat. Once melted, turn the heat off and add the chocolate chips. Move the pan to a cool place on the cooker and whisk together the cocoa powder, coconut milk and honey. Let the mixture cool to room temperature. Then spoon over your favourite cake or cupcakes. Use an angled cake spatula to spread the icing evenly.

Strudel

A **strudel** is a type of layered pastry with a (usually sweet) filling. It became popular in the 18th century throughout the Habsburg Empire. Strudel is part of Austrian cuisine but is also common in other Central European cuisines.

The oldest strudel recipes (a Millirahmstrudel and a turnip strudel) are from 1696, in a handwritten cookbook at the Wienbibliothek im Rathaus (formerly Wiener Stadtbibliothek). The pastry is descended from similar Near Eastern pastries.

The best-known strudels are apple strudel (Apfelstrudel in German) and topfenstrudel (with sweet soft quark cheese, in Austrian German topfen), followed by the Millirahmstrudel (milk-cream strudel, milchrahmstrudel). Other strudel types include sour cherry (weichselstrudel), sweet cherry, nut filled (nussstrudel), apricot strudel, plum strudel, poppy seed strudel (mohnstrudel), and raisin strudel.

Strudel dough

Ingredients for 1 strudel

250g	Flour
30g	Oil
100g	Water
	Salt

Preparation

Mix all the ingredients into a smooth dough. Then place the
finished dough in a freezer bag, add a little oil into the bag and
coat the dough with the oil. Leave to rest in the refrigerator
overnight. This is the perfect dough for Apple Strudel.

Strudel filling for watery fruits

Ingredients for 1 strudel

5	Egg yolk
50g	Sugar
	Cinnamon, Lemon
50g	Flour
50g	Hazelnuts grated
5	Egg white
50g	Sugar

Preparation

Beat the egg yolks, sugar, cinnamon and lemon until the mixture
has a thick, light-yellow consistency.
Beat the egg whites until stiff and finally let the sugar trickle in
and beat a little more. Add the egg yolk mixture to the stiffly
beaten egg whites and finally carefully fold in the flour and
hazelnuts.
This mixture is used for watery fruits such as cherries or currants.
It is spread on the strudel dough and the fruits are spread on top.

Apple strudel

Apple strudel (German *Apfelstrudel*) is a traditional Viennese strudel, which is a popular pastry in Austria, Bavaria, the Czech Republic, Northern Italy and in many other countries in Europe that once belonged to the Austro-Hungarian Empire (1867–1918).

Oven temperature 180° C **Baking time** 45 - 60 minutes

Ingredients for 1 strudel

Strudel dough
 1 recipe of Strudel dough

Apple Filling
2 kg	Apples
200 g	Walnuts
100 g	Sugar
some	Cinnamon
1	Lemon grated

Preparation
Pile the flour on a baking (pastry) board or table and make a well in the middle, add 2 tablespoons of oil, the egg and a pinch of salt. From the edge, mix the ingredients and knead very vigorously to form an elastic, smooth dough, gradually adding about 100 ml of lukewarm water, shape into a ball and brush with oil. Cover and leave to rest in a warm place for about half an hour, this is very important so that the dough remains elastic and can be easily stretched!

Peel apples, cut into quarters, remove core and cut into thin slices, place in a bowl. Mix with grated lemon zest, 2 tablespoons lemon juice, walnuts, sugar and cinnamon.

Dust a large kitchen towel with flour, place each dough ball on it, first flatten and then roll out with the rolling pin until the pattern of the kitchen towel is clearly visible.
If it is still not thin enough, stretch the dough, by placing both hands under the kitchen towel and pulling outwards in all directions. Spread a thin layer of melted butter on the dough,

sprinkle with breadcrumbs and spread the apple mixture evenly on top.
Leave a 2 - 3 cm wide margin on both narrow sides and one long side, fold in the narrow sides up to the filling. Then, from the side that has not been cut out, roll it up quickly with the help of the kitchen towel. Place the rolls on the greased baking tray or on the baking tray lined with baking paper. The seam should come down so that it does not rise. Now brush the surface of the strudel with plenty of melted butter and then bake it at 180 degrees top/bottom in a preheated oven for about 1 hour
Leave to cool slightly and dust with icing sugar, served with cream or custard.

Bienenstich with Butter Vanilla Cream

The origin of the name "Bienenstich" is unclear, but according to the "baker's boy legend," the inhabitants of Linz on the Rhine planned an attack on the neighboring town of Andernach (because the emperor had withdrawn the Rhine toll from the people of Linz and awarded it to the people of Andernach). One morning in the year 1474, two Andernach baker's apprentices were walking along the town wall and eating honey from the bees' nests that were hanging there. When they saw the attackers, they threw the bee nests at them, so that the Linzers - stung by the bees - had to flee. To celebrate, a special cake was baked - the bee sting. In the text of the baker's boy saga by Karl Simmrock, however, there is no reference to the bee sting. The earliest reference from Google Books (as of 2021) in which the baker's boy saga is directly associated with the invention of the "bee sting cake" dates back to 1962.

Oven temperature 180° C **Baking time** about 25 minutes

Ingredients for 1 tray

Yeast dough

500 g	Flour
1	Yeast cube
100 g	Sugar
1 pack	Vanilla sugar
1 pinch	Salt
250 ml	Milk
100 g	Soft Butter

Topping

150 g	Butter
1 pck.	Vanilla sugar
100 g	Sugar
30 ml	Honey
50 ml	Cream
200 g	Sliced almonds
100 g	Ground almonds

Filling

150 g	Vanilla pudding powder
120 g	Sugar
1,5 l	Milk
300 g	Butter

Preparation:

Sift the flour into a bowl, make a well and add the yeast, milk and sugar. Stir with a little flour to form a pre-dough. Cover with flour and let rise in a warm place for about 15 minutes.

Mix the remaining dough ingredients into the pre-dough and knead vigorously for about 10 minutes.

Cover the dough and let it rise in a warm place for about 30 minutes to double in volume.

For the topping, heat the butter, sugar and cream. Add the flaked almonds and bring to the boil once.

Knead the dough again, then roll it out on a floured work surface. Place on a baking tray lined with baking paper and brush with the almond mixture. Bake in a preheated oven at 180°C for approx. 25 minutes. Leave to cool on a cooling rack. For the filling, cook a pudding from pudding powder, sugar and milk according to package instructions and stir the butter into the hot pudding, cover and allow to cool.

Cut the cake crosswise.

Spread the bottom cake layer with cream and place the top cake layer on top.

Austrian Poppy Seed Cake

Oven temperature *160° - 180° C* **Baking time** *about 60 minutes*

Ingredients

8	Egg yolks
300 g	Butter
300 g	Sugar
300 g	Ground Poppy Seed
75 g	citronade
12	Egg whites- to snow

Preparation

Cream the butter and sugar until fluffy. Stir in one egg yolk at a time. Stir in the grated poppy seeds. Beat the egg whites and salt until stiff and fold into the poppy seed mixture.

Fill the dough into a greased spring-form pan (26 - 28 cm). Bake in a preheated oven at 160 - 180°C for about 60 minutes. After cooling, sprinkle with icing sugar.

Baked Cheesecake

The earliest known literary records of a cheesecake come from Athenaios, a colourful writer in antiquity. Athenaios' works are among the most important sources for ancient cuisine, as he also refers to many other writers whose works, however, have been lost.

Finally, Athenaios quotes Kallimachos, who is considered the founder of scientific philology. Kallimachos had mentioned several writings with cheesecake recipes, including one by Aigimios, presumably a Greek physician, a writing concerning cake-making. Aigimios, like Hippocrates, probably lived between the 5th and 4th centuries BC.
For the same period, the popularity of a cheesecake made from curd or sour cream is attested in ancient Greece. The Romans adopted the preparation from the Greeks. Corresponding recipes have been handed down from the collection of Cato the Elder.

A recipe from the late Middle Ages comes from the 14th century French cookbook Le Viandier. The oldest modern (German-language) cheesecake recipe is found in Anna Wecker's cookbook from 1598, where she lists eggs, sugar, butter and cinnamon as ingredients in addition to curd cheese. 100 years later, the Complete Nuremberg Cookbook contains several recipes for "Eyer-Käß-Dorten".
There are numerous variations of cheesecake by adding berries or stone fruit (for example raspberries, blueberries, blackberries, red and black currants, cherries, but also sultanas) to the cheese mixture before baking. Other possibilities include adding vanilla, vanillin, lemon oil or maple syrup.

Oven temperature 160° C **Baking time** 50 - 60 minutes

Ingredients

250g	Butter
320g	Sugar
6	Eggs
2 Tbsp.	Flour
30g	Vanilla sugar
1 pck.	Custard powder
1250g	Quark

Preparation

Cream butter and sugar, then add eggs one by one. Gently stir in the quark and finally fold in the flour and custard powder. For the base, sprinkle sliced almonds into the tin and stir in the quark mixture.

Bake at 160 degrees in a preheated oven for 50 - 60 minutes. The dough must rise up in the middle.

Linzertorte

The Linzer torte is likely to be the oldest cake to be named after a town. For a long time, a recipe from 1696 in the Vienna Stadt- und Landesbibliothek was the oldest one known, but 2005, Waltraud Faißner, the library director of the Upper Austrian Landesmuseum and author of the book *Wie man die Linzer Dortten macht* ("How to make the Linzer Torte"), found an even older Veronese recipe from 1653 in the archive of Admont Abbey.

There are many legends around the Linzer torte, claiming that it was invented either by a Viennese confectioner named Linzer (as given by Alfred Polgar), or the Franconian pastry chef Johann Konrad Vogel (1796–1883), who started mass production of the cake in Linz around 1823.

The Austrian migrant Franz Hölzlhuber claimed to have introduced the Linzer torte to Milwaukee in the 1850s.

Oven temperature 180° C **Baking time** 60 minutes

Ingredients

250 g	Flour
250 g	Sugar
250 g	Butter
250 g	ground almonds
1 pck	Vanilla sugar
4	Egg yolk
2	Eggs
½ TSP	Cinnamon
Pinch	Clove powder
	Redcurrant jam for spreading

Preparation

Knead a short crust pastry from all the ingredients. Place 2/3 of the dough in a spring-form pan and spread thickly with cranberry jam. Form even rolls from the remaining dough and cover the cake with them like a grid.

Bake in a preheated oven for 60 minutes at 180°C.

Nut Striezel

In German and Austrian cuisine, Striezel is a pastry made of yeast dough similar to the French brioche. In eastern and central Germany, it is used to describe elongated baked goods made of yeast dough. It is synonymous with stollen, but cakes such as poppy seed striezel are also called stollen. In Bavaria and Austria, on the other hand, striezel is understood to mean a yeast plait, while filled yeast dough rolls are called strudel.

Oven temperature 165° C **Baking time** approx. 30 minutes

Ingredients for 1 plait
Dough

500 g	Plain flour type 480
1	Yeast cube
0,25 l	Milk
2-3	Egg yolks
½ tsp	Salt
50 g	Butter
1 p	Vanilla sugar
	Zest of one lemon
50 g	sugar

Nut filling

200 g	Walnuts grated
2 tbsp	Honey
30 g	Breadcrumbs
2 tbsp	Rum
125 ml	Milk
	Cinnamon to taste
1 egg	to coat

Preparation

Mix the milk with the water and dissolve in the yeast. Then add the salt and sugar and set the mixture aside for a short time. Mix the flour with the butter, egg and rum. Then add the yeast mixture. Knead everything well until you have a smooth dough. The best way to do this is by hand, knead for at least 10 minutes. Then leave to rise for approx. 1.5 hours in a warm place covered with a kitchen towel.

The volume should increase considerably.
Meanwhile, mix the nuts with the honey, breadcrumbs, rum and milk in a mixing bowl until homogeneous.
After the rising time, knead the dough well again and roll out on a floured surface to a rectangular shape about 1 cm thick. Spread the nut mixture over as much of the rolled-out dough as possible. Now roll up the dough from the long side and close the ends well. Using a sharp knife, slit lengthwise (creating 2 open strands) and carefully wrap the two strands tightly around each other. Place in a greased spring-form pan and tie the ends together. Cover and leave to rise again in a warm place for about 30 minutes until the volume has increased considerably.
Preheat the oven to 165 degrees Celsius. Sprinkle the dough with sugar and cinnamon if you like (it holds especially well if you moisten the dough with a little water beforehand) and bake for approx. 30 minutes on the middle shelf.

Carrot Cake

The origins of carrot cake are disputed.
In volume two of *L'art du cuisinier* (1814), Antoine Beauvilliers,
former chef to Louis XVI, wrote a recipe for a "Gâteau de Carottes",
which was copied verbatim in some competitors' cookbooks.
In 1824, Beauvilliers published an English version of his cookbook in
London which includes a recipe for "Carrot Cakes" in a literal
translation of his earlier recipe.
The housekeeping school of Kaiseraugst (Canton of Aargau,
Switzerland) has a similar 19th-century recipe - it is one of the most
popular cakes in Switzerland, especially for children's' birthdays,
according to the Culinary Heritage of Switzerland.

The popularity of carrot cake was revived in the United Kingdom
because of rationing during the Second World War.

Oven temperature 175° C **Baking time** about 60 minutes

Ingredients

340 g	Sugar
7	Eggs
1½ TSP.	Lemon zest
400 g	Carrots
400 g	Almonds / hazelnuts
90 g	Flour
2 TSP.	Baking powder, salt and vanilla

Casting

1	Lemon juice
250 g	Icing sugar
12	Marzipan carrots

Preparation

Peel the carrots and grate finely. Separate the eggs.
Beat the egg yolks until white and foamy, slowly adding the sugar.
Beat the egg whites until stiff and let them slide onto the yolks.
Add the carrots, nuts, cinnamon, flour and baking powder. Mix
everything loosely with the dough scraper.

Preheat the oven to 175°C. Cover the bottom of a spring-form pan (26 cm) with baking paper.

Pour in the dough and bake on the middle shelf at 175°C top and bottom heat for 1 hour.

For the decoration, mix the icing sugar with the lemon juice. Spread the icing on the cake. Place the marzipan carrots in the icing and finally sprinkle the chopped pistachios over the cake.

The cake is nice and moist and tastes very nutty!

Sachertorte

Forerunners of the Sacher cake can already be found in the 18th century, for example in Conrad Hagger's cookbook (1718) or in Gartler-Hickmann's "Wienerisches bewährtem Kochbuch" (1749).

In 1832 Prince Metternich commissioned his court kitchen to create a special dessert for his high-ranking guests – this was beginning of the Sachertorte story. "Don't let him disgrace me tonight!" he said. But the head chef was ill and so the 16-year-old apprentice Franz Sacher (1816-1907), had to take on the task and in the process invented the Sacher Torte.
Although the cake apparently pleased the guests very much, no further attention was paid to it. After years in Pressburg and Budapest, Franz Sacher returned to Vienna in 1848, where he opened a delicatessen and wine shop.
His eldest son Eduard (1843-1892) trained with the Imperial and Royal Court confectioner Demel and during this time completed the Sacher Torte in the form we know today. The Sacher Torte was first offered at Demel and then also at the Hotel Sacher, which Eduard founded in 1876. Since then, the cake has been considered one of Vienna's most famous culinary specialties.

Oven temperature *170° C* **Baking time** *about 45 minutes*

Ingredients for 1 spring-form pan 24 cm Ø (12 pieces)

130 g	Dark chocolate 70%
6	Eggs (size M)
130 g	Soft butter
130 g	Flour
200 g	Dark chocolate 70%
½	Vanilla bean
Pinch	Salt
110 g	Sugar
200 g	Apricots jam
1 TBSP.	Sunflower or other neutral oil

Preparation

Preheat the oven to 170°. Line the bottom of the pan with baking paper.
For the dough, break the chocolate into pieces, melt over a hot water bath and leave to cool to finger warm.

Slit the vanilla pod in half lengthwise and scrape out the pith with
a knife. Separate the eggs.
Beat the egg whites with 1 pinch of salt until stiff.
Cream the butter with the sugar and vanilla pulp with the whisks
of a hand mixer until the sugar has completely dissolved.
First, gradually stir in the egg yolks, then the cooled chocolate.
Gently mix the beaten egg whites together with the sifted flour into
the butter mixture using a spatula.
Pour the dough into the tin, smooth down and bake in a hot oven
(centre, fan oven 150°) for approx. 45 min. Then leave to rest for
approx. 15 min. in the switched-off oven. Remove the finished cake,
leave to cool for 5 minutes, carefully remove from the tin and the
baking paper, place on a wire rack using a cake lifter and leave to
cool.
For the filling and garnish, heat the jam briefly in a saucepan.
Cut the cake once crosswise. Spread the bottom layer with half of
the jam.
Assemble the cake, brush all around with the remaining jam and
let it soak in for at least 2 hours.
Break the dark chocolate into pieces and melt over a hot water
bath. Mix with the oil and leave to cool until warm to the touch.
Place a grid on a sheet of baking paper or a baking tray. Place the
cake on it.
Pour the chocolate over the cake and spread it smoothly all
around. Chill the cake for at least 3 hours before serving.

Baumkuchentorte

The exact date when Baumkuchen was invented is not known.
Some historians believe that the Baumkuchen is of Hungarian
origin. It was a kind of wedding cake and quickly found its way
into German cuisine. Others, however, claim that a similar form
was already known to the ancient Greeks.
The first recipes for the cake can be found in an Italian cookbook
from 1426. The name "Baumkuchen" was first used in 1682 in a
cookbook written by Johann Sigismund Elsholtz, Elector Friedrich
Wilhelm of Brandenburg's personal physician. The oldest surviving
recipe in German appeared around 1450 in a Heidelberg
manuscript. In Nuremberg and Frankfurt am Main, Baumkuchen
was already a well-known wedding cake of the patricians in the
15th century.

In the 16th century, the production method changed; the cake
dough was now no longer laid in a ring around a rotating wooden
roller, but as a whole piece and tied tightly with strings. The
typical indentations of the Baumkuchen were created by the
binding. In the 17th century, another new production method
emerged in which the thin liquid mixture was applied in layers to
the rotating roller. At this time, it also became common to apply a
glaze of sugar and rose water. However, sugar was still used
rather sparingly in the preparation of the mixture at this time;
nutmeg, cinnamon and cardamom were used for seasoning.
The recipe used today was not developed until the 18th century.
One of the first known recipes of this new type is contained in the
7th edition of the Nieder-Sächsisches Koch-Buch of 1758. At that
time, the finished Baumkuchen was sprinkled with grated
chocolate or completely coated with couverture. From about 1800
onwards, these cakes were hardly ever made in private households,
but almost exclusively by confectioners. Baumkuchen was mainly
baked in Berlin in the first half of the 19th century, with migrants
from French-speaking Switzerland, such as Josty, Spargnapani or
d'Heureuse, making their mark on the market. The absorptive
power of the Berlin market allowed mail-order bakeries in
Dresden, Cottbus, Stettin and Salzwedel to sell their local specialties
from the 1870s onwards. Salzwedeler Baumkuchen has

had the EU quality mark of "protected geographical indication"
since 2010.
In the late 18th century, Baumkuchen, which was often presented
by aristocrats at ceremonial tables, became a dish of the upper
middle classes in the 19th century. In Central Germany,
Brandenburg, Mecklenburg and Pomerania it became a
representative wedding dish. In the second half of the 19th century,
Baumkuchen was also served at Easter, New Year's Eve and larger
family celebrations.

In the late 19th century, it increasingly became a typical German
cake, also part of the Bismarck cult. At the same time, simpler
variants such as the Baumkuchentorte, the Bismarck Oak or the
Baumkuchenspitzen began to spread to the middle classes. New
ovens powered by gas and then also by electricity also led to
cheaper confectionery, from which the mail-order bakeries
profited.

The Bumkuchentorte is a variation of the original Baumkuchen
(tree cake).

Oven temperature 180° C

Ingredients for 1 cake

200 g	Butter
175 g	Sugar
265 g	Egg white
125 g	Sugar
175 g	Egg yolks
175 g	Starch powder
65 g	Roasted almond semolina
2,5 g	Salt
5 cl	Arrack and tonka bean
1	Grated lemon peel
2-3	Vanilla pods
	Apricot jam
200g	Chocolate coating
50g	Coconut oil

Preparation

Separate the eggs. Cream butter and sugar.
Beat the egg whites until stiff and gradually add the sugar.
Gradually stir the egg yolks into the egg whites.
Slit the vanilla pods in half lengthwise and scrape out the pulp.

Add to the fat together with the grated almonds, arrack, grated lemon and tonka bean. Then stir in the flour.
Finally, fold the egg whites into the batter.

Line the bottom of a spring-form pan (28 cm diameter) with parchment paper.

Spread 3 tablespoons of the dough on the bottom of the tin. Bake under the grill or in a preheated oven at 175 °C top heat/bottom heat on the highest setting until light yellow. Repeat until all the batter has been used up.
Leave to cool in the moulds. Carefully loosen the cake with a knife at the edge of the tin, turn out onto a cooling rack and remove the paper.

Heat the jam and pass through a sieve. Brush the edge and surface of the larger cake with it.
Melt the couverture with the coconut oil in a bain-marie and coat the cake with it.
Leave the cake well wrapped in a cool place for at least a week before serving.

French chocolate cake

Oven temperature 175° C **Baking time** 30 - 35 minutes

Ingredients for 16 pieces

500 g	Dark chocolate
125 g	Butter
6	Eggs (M)
100 g	Icing sugar
½	Vanilla pod
125 ml	Double cream (alternatively whipped cream)

Preparation

Chop the chocolate. Dice the butter. Melt together over a hot water bath. Take down, stir until smooth and leave to cool slightly. Separate the eggs. Beat the egg whites until just stiff and set aside. Sieve the icing sugar and whisk with the egg yolks and vanilla pulp until thick and pale. Stir in the double cream or cream. Gradually add the cooled chocolate mixture and beat in. Fold in the beaten egg whites in 3 portions.Pour the batter into a greased, floured spring-form pan (26 cm diameter). Bake in a preheated oven at 175 °C for 30-35 minutes until the surface is just firm.

Do not bake the cake too long, the centre should still be a little soft. Remove the cake from the oven and allow to cool on a cooling rack. Then cover well with aluminium foil and leave to cool for at least 1 day. Remove the cake from the tin, and dust with icing sugar before serving. Serve with whipped cream or vanilla ice cream and fresh berries.

Engadine nut cake

The history of this nut cake is a story of exchange and inspiration.
At the end of the 19th century, many Grisons bakers and
confectioners emigrated to find work in Europe. Two of them,
Heinz & Tester, founded a confectionery in Toulouse, France. The
Graubünden confectioners were inspired by the traditional nut
cake recipes in the south of France, especially the Tarte aux noix
du Périgord, which, however, has no top and therefore has a
shorter shelf life. Le Bourianoix, also a Périgord specialty, is very
close to the nut tart. Fausto Pult also worked in this confectionery,
who later returned to Samedan and began to produce and sell the
Engadine nut tart under the name "Pulttorte" in his bakery-
confectionery from 1926. He reaped great success for his cake in
1934 when he presented it to a wider public at the Basel Sample
Fair.
As the climate is less suitable for walnut trees in some mountain
valleys in Graubünden, the walnuts were imported. According to
one theory, Graubünden emigrants brought walnut trees from
France back to their homeland, where they still grow in Bergell.

Oven temperature 175° C **Baking time** about 55 minutes

Ingredients for 1 cake

For the dough

400 g	Flour
180 g	Sugar
1 pinch	Salt
1 TSP.	Lemon zest
1	Egg
200 g	Butter

For the filling

250 g	Sugar
300 ml	Cream at least 30 % fat content
4 Tbsp.	Honey
400 g	chopped hazelnuts
1 cl	Kirsch

Also

	Butter for the mold
1	Egg yolk
1 TBSP.	Milk
	Powdered sugar to dust

Preparation

Dough

For the dough Heap the flour with the sugar, salt and lemon zest onto a work surface, make a well in the middle, beat in the egg and spread the butter in flakes around the well. Chop all the ingredients with a knife until crumbly and work quickly with your hands to make a smooth dough. Shape into a ball and wrap in cling film and place in the fridge for 30 minutes.

Filling

For the filling, melt the sugar in a saucepan over low heat, add the cream and honey while stirring, bring to the boil, add the nuts and cherry brandy and allow everything to cool.

Preheat oven to 175 degrees.
Roll out a good 1/3 of the dough on a floured work surface, line the tin with it and form a 2 cm high rim. Spread the nut mixture over the base. Roll out 1/3 of the dough to the size of the mould and cover the nut mixture with it. Roll out the remaining dough thinly, cut out strips about 1.5 cm wide and place a grid on top of the cake. Mix the egg yolk with the milk and brush the surface with it. Bake in a preheated oven for about 45 minutes. Cover with aluminium foil for the last 10 minutes. Serve dusted with icing sugar and cut into pieces.

Spanish Orange Almond Cake (Gluten free)

Oven temperature 180° C **Baking time** 25 - 40 minutes

Ingredients

2	Oranges, approx. 280 g,
5	Eggs, separated
200 g	Icing sugar
225 g	Ground almonds
2 Tbsp.	Flaked almonds
	Sifted icing sugar for decorating

Ingredients

Place the chopped oranges with skin in a small saucepan and remove all the seeds. Add 1 tablespoon of water, cover and cook gently for 30 minutes or until the oranges are soft and excess liquid has evaporated. Allow to cool.

Preheat the oven to 180 ° C (350 ° F, gas mark 4). Line the bottom and sides of a 23 cm spring-form pan with baking paper.

Finely chop the oranges with a large knife or in a food processor or blender.

Place the egg whites in a large bowl and beat until they form stiff peaks. Gradually whisk in half the powdered sugar and beat for 1 minute. Using the same whisk, whisk the egg yolks with the remaining sugar in another bowl for 2-3 minutes, or until pale and fairly thick.

Gently fold in the finely chopped orange mixture and ground almonds.

Stir in 3 tablespoons of fully beaten egg white to loosen the mixture, and gently fold in the remaining white with a large metal spoon.

Transfer the mixture to the prepared tin and level the top. Sprinkle with the flaked almonds.

Bake for 50-55 minutes or until the cake is golden and a skewer inserted into the center comes out clean. Check the cake after 20 minutes and again after 30 minutes and cover lightly with foil if it is browning too quickly. Leave the cake to cool in the tin, then turn off the baking paper and transfer to a cake plate. Dust with icing sugar before serving.

The cake can be stored in an airtight tin for up to 2 days.

Zwetschgenkuchen (Damson Plum Flan)

Zwetschgenkuchen, also known as **Pflaumenkuchen**, **Zwetschgendatschi** (Bavaria and Austria) or **Zwetschgenplootz** (Franconia) is a sheet cake or pie made from yeast dough or shortcrust dough that is thinly spread onto a baking sheet or other baking mould and covered with pitted damson plums. It is popular as a summer cake and has different local names throughout Germany, Austria and Switzerland.
In Hessen, Rhineland-Palatinate, Saarland and Moselle it is known as Quetschekuche.
In Bavaria, Baden-Württemberg and parts of Austria it is called Zwetschgendatschi and in Rhineland and the Eifel Prummetaat. "Datschi" is thought to be derived from the dialect word "detschen" or "datschen" that can be translated as "pinching" (as the plums are pinched into the dough). Made with shortcrust pastry, it is common to serve it with Streusel (a crumbly mixture of butter, sugar and flour) although the original recipe serves it plain without any toppings. There are claims that the cake was invented in Augsburg where it is considered the city's signature dish. It is said that it resembles the "Zirbelnuss", the city's coat of arms, and from this association Augsburg is also nicknamed "Datschiburg".
In the Palatinate and Rhenish Hesse, it is eaten with potato soup or vegetable soup as a main dish for lunch. In contrast the people in Saarland eat it with bean soup and call this dish "Bibbelschesbohnesup un Quetschekuche".

Oven temperature 160° C **Baking time** about 50 minutes

Ingredients for 1 tray

Dough

200 g	Curd/Quark
6 Tbsp.	Milk
1	Egg
3 TBSP.	Oil
1	Vanilla sugar
400 g	Flour
4 P	Baking powder

Topping
1,5 Kg   Damson plums

Casting
100 g   Sugar
2   Eggs
250 ml   Sour cream
         Cinnamon

Preparation
Make a quark oil dough from the dough ingredients.
Mix all ingredients to a smooth dough. Distribute the pitted plums evenly on the dough.
Bake the cake at 160° C convection oven
Pour the glaze over the top after 20 minutes of baking and bake for another 30 minutes.

Gateaux

Who cannot love delicious Gateaux?
Whether it's buttercream or cream pies that make your mouth water,
melt in your mouth. Here is something for every taste.

Buttercream Gateaux

Cream Gateaux

Frankfurter Kranz

The Frankfurt wreath, with its round shape and brittle covering, is the image of a crown of the German emperors, which is supposed to remind us of Frankfurt am Main as the place of coronation. In addition, there are the voucher cherries, which symbolise rubies. It was created around 1735, the oldest surviving recipe dates from the beginning of the 20th century.

In English, the cake is therefore also called Frankfurt Crown Cake, while in French it is known as Couronne de Francfort, Frankfurter Krone.[1] The cake is also called Frankfurt Crown Cake.

Oven temperature 180° C **Baking time** about 40 - 50 minutes
Total time about 2 hours

Preparation for 1 wreath

Sponge

300 g	Sugar
300 g	Butter
420 g	Whole egg
220 g	Starch
220 g	Flour
15 g	Baking powder

Buttercream filling

1000g butter

1 l	Milk
2	Vanilla pudding powder
100g	Sugar

Brittle

300 g	Sugar
350 g	Almond slivers
	Redcurrant jelly, cherries inlay

Preparation

Mix the softened butter with the sugar until creamy add the lemon zest and the salt and mix well add the flour, cornflour and baking powder and stir until everything is well mixed pour the batter into the prepared wreath form.
Bake in a preheated oven for about 40 - 50 minutes at 180 degrees. Allow to cool on a cake rack

Buttercream

Make a pudding from the milk, pudding powder and 100 g sugar, leave to cool, stirring occasionally. Cream the soft butter and then add the cooled pudding by the spoonful, mixing everything together well.

Almond brittle

For the brittle, caramelize the sugar, add the almond slivers and mix everything together until the almond slivers are covered by the sugar mixture. Leave to cool on an oiled baking tray. Put the brittle in a plastic bag and roll over it with a rolling pin to crush it.

Completion

Cut the cake base three times horizontally. Put some of the cream in a piping bag and spread the bases first with redcurrant jelly and then with buttercream. Put the last base on top and then spread the cake with the remaining buttercream and then sprinkle the Frankfurter Kranz all around with the brittle. Pipe dots of cream on top and place the candied cherries on top to finish.
Now place the cake in the refrigerator for at least 2 hours before cutting.

Prince Regent Gateaux

The Prinzregententorte is named after the Prince Regent Prince Luitpold of Bavaria, who first led the Bavarian government for his incapacitated nephew King Ludwig II of Bavaria (the "Castle King"), and then for his sick brother King Otto I of Bavaria, for 26 years.

Oven temperature 160° C **Baking time** 6 – 8 minutes per base
Total time about 2 hours

Ingredients

Thin Sponge base

9	Egg white
85 g	Sugar
6	Egg yolk
225 g	Sugar
255 g	Flour
60 g	Cornstarch
10 g	Baking powder

French Buttercream

315 g	Icing sugar	
500 g	Butter	>>> beat until creamy
250 g	Whole egg	
125 g	Egg yolk	>>> add eggs and egg yolks little by little
125 g	Coconut oil	
315 g	Chocolate coating	>>> melt both and add to the buttercream
	Rum	

Casting

200g	Chocolate coating
50g	Coconut oil

Preparation

Sponge cake bases

For the sponge dough, mix flour, powder/cornstarch and baking powder and sift.

Beat egg yolks and sugar first, warm over steam, with a whisk until foamy. When the mixture has reached about 40 degrees, take off the heat and beat with a mixer until cold. It then has a light yellow almost white color.

Beat the egg whites until stiff and let the sugar trickle in at the end.

First, gently fold the egg whites into the egg yolk mixture. Gently fold in the flour mixture one tablespoon at a time.

Place the 7 sheets of baking paper next to each other and portion the dough evenly on the sheets. Place a 26 cm spring-form border around the pastry on the first sheet of baking paper and spread the pastry evenly with the back inside the ring using a small, angled palette. Prepare the remaining cake layers in the same way.

Bake in a preheated oven at 160 degrees convection oven for about 6-8 minutes. Then immediately separate the bases from the baking paper and let the cake bases cool individually on the baking paper.

Buttercream

To make the buttercream, cream together the butter and icing sugar until the butter is a whitish colour. The eggs are added little by little. The chocolate coating is melted with the coconut oil and finally stirred into the buttercream. Be careful - it may be almost cold but still liquid. Slowly fold into the cream in small portions.

Completion

To assemble the Prinzregententorte, spread the bottom cake layer thinly with buttercream. Then place the next cake layer on top and spread a thin layer of buttercream.

Proceed in the same way with the remaining layers but place the top layer face down to create a flat surface. Coat the Prince Regent cake with the remaining buttercream, first around the edges and then on top, using a wide knife or a palette. Then place the Prince Regent cake in the fridge for about an hour to allow the buttercream to set before applying the chocolate icing.

Cast

For the chocolate icing, chop 200 g of couverture and heat in a water bath while stirring to approx. 40 degrees (well lukewarm). Then remove the chocolate from the water bath and add 50 g coconut oil. Now stir until the coconut oil is melted.

Lift the Prinzregententorte with a palette onto a cake rack. Pour the chocolate onto the centre of the Prince Regent cake and spread it over the cake with the palette so that the chocolate runs down the edge of the cake. Spread the chocolate all around the edge and then refrigerate the Prinzregententorte again.

When the chocolate frosting is set, heat the blade of a knife on the stovetop and use it to mark cake pieces on the cake frosting and use the blade to press grooves into the frosting, on top and around the edge of the cake, so the frosting doesn't break later when you cut it.

Have fun baking your Prince Regent cake!

Buckwheat cranberry Gateaux

Oven temperature 160° - 180° C **Baking time** about 30 minutes

Ingredients

Sponge cake base

2 whole	Eggs
3 egg	Yolks
3 egg	Whites
175 g	Sugar
1 tsp	Vanilla sugar
170 g	Buckwheat flour
2 tsp	Cream of tartar baking powder
1	Pinch of salt
3 tbsp	Cold water

Filling

400 g	Cranberries
some	Raspberry jam
700 ml	Cream
1 tbsp	Vanilla sugar
Pinch of salt	

To decorate

100 g	Flaked almonds,
2 tbsp	Chopped hazelnuts or

brittle to taste (chocolate sprinkles will also work, of
      course)

Preparation

First toast the almond flakes in a pan without fat. Leave to cool.
For the cake mixture, beat the 2 whole eggs and the 3 egg yolks
with the sugar, vanilla sugar and water for about 10 minutes until
foamy.
Mix the buckwheat flour with the baking powder and sift over the
egg mixture and gently fold in. Beat the egg whites with a pinch of
salt until stiff, and fold into the batter.
Bake at 160 degrees Celsius in a fan oven, or 180 degrees Celsius top
and bottom heat for about 30 minutes on the middle shelf. Use a
wooden stick or knitting needle to check whether the dough is
ready.

If it is too dark, cover with aluminium foil after 25 minutes.
Allow to cool.

Filling

For the filling, whip 400 ml cream with vanilla sugar and salt
until very stiff. Carefully mix the whipped cream into the
cranberries. Refrigerate. Whip 300 ml cream until stiff. Fill about
a third into a bag with a piping bag. Put everything in a cool
place.

Slice the baked cake twice horizontally. Spread a layer of
raspberry jam on the first cake layer and then spread a third of
the cranberry cream on top.

Place the second cake layer on top and spread the second third of
the filling. Spread a thin layer of raspberry jam on the underside of
the third base, place it on top and spread the rest of the filling on
the top of the cake.

Brush the edge of the cake with whipped cream. This is best done
with a pastry spatula. Then use the pastry spatula to "stick" the
almond flakes into the cream for the edge of the cake.

Decorate the cake with the cream in a piping bag and decorate
with chopped hazelnuts, brittle or chocolate sprinkles as desired.

Viennese Mixture / Sponge base

Viennese sponge base is a fine baked product made from a Viennese mixture. It is similar to sponge cake, to which liquid fat is added. Viennese mixture is also called "light sand mixture".
To make a Viennese mixture, whisk eggs, sugar, salt and flavourings over a bain-marie to form a basic mixture, which is then cooled while being stirred constantly. Now fold in wheat flour and starch powder. In contrast to sponge cake, liquid fat such as melted butter or heated vegetable oil is then added. The fat content makes the Viennese mixtures finer pored and juicier than sponge cake mixtures and they stay fresh longer. To prevent the whipped air from escaping, Viennese mixtures must be baked immediately. Then bake the Viennese mixture in a spring-form pan and use the finished cake base for layer cakes such as buttercream cakes, cream cakes or cut into pieces as a base for fruit cakes.

Viennese sponge base

Oven temperature 180° C **Baking time** approx. 30 -40 minutes

Ingredients for 1 high spring-form pan (28 cm Ø)

15	Eggs size M, separated
450 g	Finest sugar
3 Tbsp	Vanilla sugar
	Grated zest of an organic lemon
300 g	Wheat flour type 405 or 550
150	Starch
225 g	Butter, melted lukewarm

Preparation

Beat the egg whites with a hand mixer until stiff, but not firm, while letting the sugar trickle in. Mix in the beaten egg yolks with the vanilla sugar or/and the lemon zest. Mix the l the cornflour, sieve onto the egg foam and fold in alternately with the melted butter. Pour the mixture into the prepared spring-form pan (26 cm Ø), smooth out and bake immediately in the preheated oven (180° C, top/bottom heat) for about 20-25 minutes. You can use this Sponge to create a Gateau to your taste and desire ;)

Champagne cake with limes

Ingredients

Sponge
see Viennese sponge base

Filling

100 g	Lemon jelly
2	Untreated lemons
50 ml	Water
125 g	Sugar
2	Egg yolk
8	Soaked white gelatine leaves
2	Piccolo bottles of sparkling wine
80 ml	Lime juice
600 ml	Whip cream
1 sachet	Vanilla sugar
1	Lime

Preparation

Make a sponge cake base about 2-3 cm thick. Heat the jelly and brush the sponge cake base with it, then place the base in the spring-form pan.

Wash the lemons, peel them thinly and boil the peel with water, cover with 100 g sugar and boil for 15 minutes.

Take out the peel and add the egg yolks to the liquid.

Squeeze out the soaked gelatine leaves and melt them one by one in the hot liquid. Allow the mixture to cool slightly, add the sparkling wine and stir in the lime or lemon juice and a little sugar, then refrigerate.

Whip the cream until stiff and season with the remaining sugar and vanilla sugar. Spread about ¾ of this into the gelling mixture and pour the cream onto the sponge cake base.

Smooth the surface with the pastry card or a pastry scraper and cover the cake and refrigerate for 4-5 hours.

Take the cake out of the springform pan and pipe the remaining cream onto the cake as cream curls.

Cut 4 very thin lime slices, quarter them and place them on the cream curls.

Egg liqueur Gateau

Ingredients

Sponge
See Viennese sponge base

Filling
3 pck.	Cream stiffener
1 pck.	Vanilla sugar
700 g	Whipped cream
200 ml	eggnog
1-2 Tbsp	dark chocolate chips

Preparation
Cut the sponge cake into two layers, each layer about 2-3 cm thick. Mix cream stiffener and vanilla sugar, stir into the cream and whip until stiff. Remove 250 g of cream and fold in 4 tablespoons of advocaat. Spread the egg liqueur cream on the bottom sponge cake, place the top sponge cake layer on top.

Place 4 tablespoons of cream in a piping bag with a star-shaped nozzle. Cover the cake all around with the remaining cream. Then pipe dots close together around the top edge of the cake so that no gaps remain. Carefully pour the remaining eggnog into the middle of the cake. Decorate cake with chocolate shavings and refrigerate until ready to serve.

Tip for fruit fans: first fill the bottom sponge with cranberries from tjar, then with egg liqueur cream.

Cheese Cream Cake

Ingredients

Base
see recipe Viennese sponge cake

Shortcrust pastry
200 g	Flour
60 g	Icing sugar
1 M	Egg
1	Pinch of salt
120 g	Cold butter

For the cream:

8 sheets	White gelatine
200 ml	Milk
125 g	Sugar
1 tsp	Lemon zest
4 M	Egg yolks
500 g	Low-fat quark
2 tbsp	Lemon juice
500 g	Cream

Preparation

Make the base

Place the flour on the work surface in a heap and make a well in the middle.

Add the icing sugar, the egg and a pinch of salt. Cut the cold butter into flakes and spread them all around the edge of the flour.

Using a large knife or palette, chop all the ingredients thoroughly from the edge until irregular crumbs form. Quickly knead these crumbs with your hands into a smooth dough.

Shape the dough into a ball, wrap in cling film, flatten slightly and chill for 30 minutes.

Preheat the oven to 180° (fan oven 160°).

Roll out a base of approx. 26 cm diameter from the shortcrust pastry and then bake until light brown.

Filling

For the cream, soak the gelatine in cold water. Boil the milk, sugar and lemon zest. Whisk 3 tbsp. of it with the egg yolks, stir the mixture into the milk. Heat, stirring constantly, until the cream thickens slightly.

Squeeze out the gelatine and dissolve it in. Pour the cream through a sieve and leave to cool. Stir the quark and lemon juice into the cold cream. Whip the cream until stiff and fold into the quark cream.

Divide the sponge cake base so that one base is approx. 3 cm thick.

Spread the apricot jam on the short pastry base and place one base on top. Then enclose it tightly with a cake ring.

Spread the curd cream on top.

Cut the other base into 16 equal pieces.

Chill the cake for at least 4 hours. Cover with the cake base cut into pieces and sprinkle the cake with icing sugar.

Lime Mascarpone Gateau

Ingredients

Crumble base
300 g	Butter biscuits
120 g	Butter

Filling
150 g	Sugar
2 TBSP.	Vanilla sugar
200 ml	freshly squeezed lime juice
16 sheets	Gelatine
2	Limes grated
300 g	Mascarpone
300 g	Yogurt 10% fat
300 g	Cream

Decoration
250 ml	Cream
	Cream stiffener and vanilla sugar to taste
2	Limes and mint or lemon balm leaves to decorate

Preparation
For the base, finely chop the butter cookies in a blender or crush them with a rolling pin.

Mix with the melted butter and press into the 28 cm diameter mold.

Refrigerate.

To make the filling, first mix the cream cheese with the yogurt, lime zest and sugar and vanilla sugar until smooth....

Soak the gelatine first, then squeeze it out and dissolve it in the warmed juice.

Stir in a little of the cream (about 3 tablespoons) so that the temperature is equalized. Then stir the mixed gelatine quickly into the cream. Refrigerate the cake for 3 hours. Remove from the ring and transfer to a cake plate. Decorate with the stiffly whipped cream and lime slices and mint.

Lübeck Nut Gateau

Oven temperature 180° C **Baking time** 20 – 30 minutes

Ingredients for 1 Sponge base

4	Egg yolk
150 g	Sugar
50 g	Marzipan
4	Egg whites - stiff
100 g	Mixed nuts
150 g	Flour
5 g	Baking powder
	Vanilla, Lemon, Salt

Preparation

Preheat oven to 180°C convection oven.
Beat egg whites with a pinch of salt until almost stiff, add 50 g
sugar and beat until completely stiff.
Beat the egg yolks with the 100 g sugar and the spices until thick.
Finally, stir in the marzipan.
Mix the nuts, flour and baking powder and stir into the egg yolks,
then fold in the beaten egg white loosely. Bake about 20 – 30
minutes until golden brown

Filling

200 g	Raspberry jam
6 TBSP.	Nut liqueur or rum (to taste)
500 g	Cream
150 g	ground hazelnuts
300 g	Cream
125 g	Hazelnut flakes

Preparation

Remove the cooled sponge cake from the mold and cut it in two
horizontally. Drizzle the bases with liqueur or rum to taste. Put
the bottom layer back into the mould. Spread with 100 g raspberry
jam.
Whip the cream with the sugar until stiff, carefully fold in the
hazelnuts.
Spread one third of it on the cake base. Place the second cake layer
on top, spread with the remaining jam and one third of the nut
cream.
Place the top layer on top, press down lightly and spread with the
remaining nut cream. Cover the cake and leave it in the fridge for
at least 1 hour.
For the decoration, briefly brown the hazelnut flakes in a pan
without fat until they begin to smell fragrant. Remove and allow
to cool.
Remove the cake from the mould.
Whip the cream until stiff. Brush the surface and the edge of the
cake with the cream and sprinkle with the hazelnut flakes.
Chill for at least 2 hours before serving.

Black Forest Gateau

The confectioner Josef Keller (1887-1981), born in the Swabian town of Riedlingen, claims to have created the Black Forest gateau for the now defunct Café Agner in the former town of Bad Godesberg, now a district of Bonn, in 1915.

A recipe written by Keller in 1927, exhibited in the Black Forest Open-Air Museum Vogtsbauernhof, had only one layer and a shortcrust pastry, in contrast to the version common today. What they have in common is the combination of cherry-cream-chocolate and the flavouring of the cream with kirsch.

The Tübingen city archivist Udo Rauch names the Tübingen master confectioner Erwin Hildenbrand of Café Walz in Tübingen as the "inventor", dated to the spring of 1930. Tübingen, which is no longer usually associated with the Black Forest, belonged to the Black Forest district from 1818 to 1924.

In 1934, the Black Forest gateau was mentioned in a book for the first time. The recipe did not call for a chocolate base, but a hazelnut shortcrust base on which cherry jam was spread before a base of walnut mixture drizzled with kirsch and sugar. On top, two rings of butter cream and a mountain of cherry cream (eggs, sugar, milk, gelatine, cream, almonds, stewed sour cherries) were spread. Finally, everything was covered with another layer of walnut mixture base. The domed top was made of cream with chocolate chips, dusted with icing sugar, just like today.

In the 1930s, the cake became known in Berlin and in confectioners' shops in major German, Austrian and Swiss cities. Before then, it was hardly possible to distribute cream cakes because there were very few electric refrigerators for storing them.

In 1949, the Black Forest gateau was the 13th best-known cake in Germany.

After that, however, its popularity developed rapidly. Today, it is the best-known and most popular cake in Germany and is known everywhere in the world.

However, in many countries some components are replaced by more local ingredients, or the alcohol is omitted.

Oven temperature 150° C convection oven / 180° C top-bottom oven
Baking time 25 – 30 minutes

Ingredients, 26cm Ø

8	Eggs (size M), room temperature and fresh
3 TBSP.	Vanilla sugar (corresponds to approx. two packets)
285 g	Sugar
175 g	Flour
60 g	Cornflour
50 g	Baking cocoa
1,5 TSP	Baking powder
2 pinch	Salt

Preparation:

Preheat the oven to 180°C top/bottom heat or 150°C convection oven!
Line the baking dish with the baking paper. Have the sieve, spatula
and cake cutter ready.
Separate the eggs and first beat the egg whites with a pinch of salt
until stiff.
Let the sugar and vanilla sugar trickle in while beating until a
silky, shiny meringue (egg white-sugar mixture) is formed.
Add the egg yolks a little at a time while the machine is running
on medium speed.
Mix flour, starch, cocoa and baking powder and sift over the
mixture.
Gently fold in with the spatula and pour into the mould. Do not
grease the edge of the mould so that the sponge does not slip off and
can climb up the edge nice and evenly!
Bake sponge mixture immediately in preheated oven for 25 to 30
minutes. Test with chopsticks!
Leave the sponge to cool on a cooling rack for ten minutes, then cut
out of the mould and leave to cool.

Filling

370 g	Sour cherries
3 Tbsp	Sugar
30 g	Cornflour
100 ml	Kirschwasser (cherry brandy)
800 g	Cream
2 packets	cream thickener
	Baking paper for the mould
50 g	Dark chocolate coating (at least 45% cocoa)

Preparation

For the filling, drain the cherries, reserving the juice.
Set aside 12 cherries.
Boil 250 ml cherry juice (add water if necessary) and 1 tbsp sugar.
Stir the starch with 5 tbsp juice or water until smooth, stir into the juice, bring to the boil once.
Stir in 1 tablespoon cherry brandy and cherries. Leave to cool.

Remove the sponge cake from the mould and divide twice horizontally. Drizzle the bases with the remaining kirsch.
Whip the cream with the remaining sugar and the cream thickener until very stiff. Place a quarter of it in a piping bag with a large star-shaped nozzle and chill.

Place the bottom cake layer in the mould and spread the cherry mixture on top. Spread thinly with cream.
Place the middle cake layer on top, spread with half of the cream and cover with the third layer. Press everything down lightly.

Remove the cake from the mould, spread the remaining cream all over and decorate with cream drops and cherries.

Grate the couverture from the block with a small knife directly onto the surface and edge of the cake. Refrigerate the cake for at least 2 hours.

Christmas is coming

Excavations and early pictorial representations prove that there was already ritual baking at festive times in pre-Christian times.

The origin of today's Christmas biscuits probably lies in the medieval monasteries.

*Exquisite baked goods were customary to commemorate the birth of
Jesus.
S
tollen was a monastic Advent pastry and recipes for gingerbread also developed in the monasteries.*

Saint Hildegard von Bingen described the positive effect of nutmeg in gingerbread and peppernuts on the mood.

Hazelnut macaroons

The first known recipe comes from the handwritten cookbook that Martha Washington's family brought with them to North America and was probably written down at the beginning of the 17th century.

This recipe uses almonds, rose water, sugar, egg white and musk. The mixture was placed on baking wafers, first baked briefly and then dried again in a lukewarm oven. Dan Jarufsky points out that the use of rose water and musk still proves the closeness to the original Arabic recipe. The first recipe that corresponds to the modern recipe and dispenses with the use of rose water and musk is found in the recipe collection of the French chef François-Pierre de La Varenne from 1652. Region-specific variants of this recipe developed in France as early as the 17th century and were often made and sold in nunneries. In Italian, maccherone at this time only referred to pasta, the similarly produced small pastry was now called amaretti (Lombardy) or marzapanetti (region around Siena).

Macaroons are a traditional Christmas biscuit in Germany. Their production has been documented since at least the 16th century, although their origin in Italy is considered likely. The term macaron has existed in the French language since that time. In 1604, a cookbook published in Liège also mentions macarons. The pastry has been known in Germany since the 17th century.

Oven temperature 150° C **Baking time** 10 - 12 minutes

Ingredients for approx. 50 macaroons

4	Egg white
200 g	Sugar
1 TBSP.	Vanilla sugar
350 g	Hazelnuts, freshly ground
	Cinnamon, bitter almond extract, Wafers
125 g	Hazelnuts, whole, for decorating

Preparation

Preheat a fan oven to 150° C.
Mix the freshly ground hazelnuts (please do not buy ground nuts!) with cinnamon and bitter almonds.

Beat the egg whites until almost stiff, carefully add the sugar a little at a time and continue to beat for about 1 minute.
Line baking trays with baking paper.

Use a piping bag to pipe small heaps, about the size of a walnut, onto the wafers. If the mixture is too thin, mix in more ground nuts if necessary.

Place a hazelnut kernel on each mound and bake for 10 - 12 minutes.

The heaps must feel dry on the outside but should still be soft on the inside. Do not let them get too dark, otherwise they taste bitter.

Rheinish Mutzen leaves

Mutzen, also Muuzen, Muze(n), are a Rhenish deep fried pastry traditionally made at carnival and New Year's Eve.

Mutzen are made from a dough of flour, eggs, sugar and flavourings. The tough dough is rolled out thinly into lozenges and fried in hot oil until golden brown. The pastry is usually dusted with icing sugar ("sweet snow").
Mutzen are mainly found in the greater Cologne area, on the Lower Rhine, in regions of the Bergisches Land, on the Middle Rhine and in the Eifel.

Oil temperature about 170° C **Baking time** about 5 minutes

Ingredients for approx. 45 Mutzen leaves

3	Chicken eggs, class M
75 g	Sugar
400 g	Flour, type 405, sifted
1 TBSP.	Vanilla sugar
40 g	Sweet cream butter, soft
1 TSP.	Lemon zest, grated
1 pinch	Sea salt
2 L	Oil for frying, e.g. peanut oil or classic Lard
	Icing sugar and vanilla sugar for sprinkling

Preparation

Beat the eggs with the granulated sugar and then fold in the flour with the other ingredients, except the icing sugar and oil, and knead in a food processor until smooth. Shape into a ball and let it rest, covered, overnight. The dough should not stick the next day. Cut the dough ball into quarters and roll out each piece of dough flat to 2 to 3 mm or turn it through the thinnest setting of the pasta machine (do not flour the dough or, if absolutely necessary, only very lightly, otherwise the frying fat will darken too quickly and give off its burnt taste to the Mutzen). Cut the dough sheets into small lozenges with the pastry wheel.
Heat the oil to approx. 170° Celsius and fry the dough pieces until they are golden brown. Sprinkle with vanilla sugar while still hot, degrease on kitchen paper and dust with icing sugar when cool.

Kourabiedes Greek nut balls with clove

Kourabiedes are a Greek Christmas biscuit similar to vanilla crescents. They are made from a crumbly dough using flour, butter, egg yolks, sugar, almonds or Walnuts and flavourings (including vanilla and clove).

Traditionally, kourabiedes come from Cappadocia, where they were prepared by local Greeks as Christmas biscuits. It was not until the early 20th century that refugees brought them to Greece. The name Kourabiés comes from the Turkish kurabiye, but originally only meant biscuits in general.

The dough is shaped into biscuits, croissants or balls (often with a whole almond or clove in the middle), baked and turned in icing sugar while still hot before the biscuits then cool.

Along with melomakarona, kourabiedes are one of the traditional Christmas pastries in Greece. However, they are available in pastry shops all year round.

Oven temperature *180° C* **Baking time** *about 20 minutes*

Ingredients for 45 cookies

225 g	soft butter
90 g	Icing sugar
2 TSP.	Vanilla paste
1	Small egg
150 g	Ground walnuts
450 g	Flour

Ornamentation

45	Whole cloves
45 g	Melted butter
	Powdered sugar

Preparation

For the dough, finely grind the walnuts - Set aside
Mix butter, icing sugar, vanilla paste and egg well.
Add flour and walnuts, and work everything into a firm dough
Cool for at least 1 hour
Preheat oven to 180 degrees top/bottom heat. Line a baking tray with baking paper

Divide the dough into 45 equal pieces and round each piece into a ball.
Put a clove in each ball and then place on the baking tray
Bake for about 20 minutes - the bottom of the cookies should turn a light brown, then they are done.
Don't be surprised, after baking they are very fragile, before you take them off the tray let them cool completely.
Immediately after removing from the oven, brush the balls with melted butter.
And immediately sprinkle with powdered sugar - now leave to cool
Packed in a tin they last about 5-6 weeks (theoretically of course).
 I can imagine them being good all year round, since it does not have a typical Christmas flavor, who knows maybe it's time to have a Greek buffet 😉

Pepparkakor - Swedish Christmas gingerbread

Pepparkakor has been eaten in Sweden since the Middle Ages, probably imported from Germany.

The delicious pastry became so popular in Sweden that Pepparkakor has even had its own holiday since 1996: 9 December. It is therefore hardly surprising that Pippi Longstocking also loved to bake Pepparkakor.

But instead of gingerbread men, she cut out horses, monkeys and big shoes from the dough - typical Pippi - but also typically Swedish. Because there are no limits to what you can do with gingerbread biscuits. Literally! For example, since 1990 there has been an annual gingerbread house exhibition at Stockholm's Ark Des Architecture and Design Museum, which is judged and awarded prizes by a panel of architecture and design experts.

Oven temperature 200° C **Baking time** 5 - 10 minutes

Ingredients:

255 g	Sugar
100 ml	Water
50 ml	Syrup, alternatively honey
½ TBSP.	Ground cinnamon
½ TBSP.	Ground cardamom
½ TBSP.	Ground ginger
½ TSP	Ground cloves
2 TBSP.	Grated orange peel
200 g	Butter
2 TSP.	Baking soda
600 g	Flour
50 ml	Cognac if required

Preparation:

Boil the water with the sugar and spices. Then cool slightly and gradually add the fat. Adults can add 50 ml of cognac. Stir vigorously until the fat is melted.

Mix the wheat flour with the baking soda and add to the sugar mixture. Quickly work into a smooth dough and refrigerate the dough until the next day

Overnight the dough becomes relatively hard, but for cutting it must be rolled out thinly on a floured work surface.
Then place the cookies on a baking tray lined with baking paper and bake at 200°C on the middle shelf for 5-10 minutes.

Speculaas

The origin of the name Spekulatius is not certain. In Low German, especially in the East Frisian language, Spikelātsje, Spekelātsje has been handed down, as well as Spekulaties in Rhenish in the 19th century. These probably go back to an 18th-century Dutch speculatie adopted in the border regions with the Netherlands, where it was first used to designate a sculpturally designed sweet, later for figurative pastries. Latinised, it became speculoos and was later interpreted as a derivative of the Latin speculum 'mirror, image'. According to Wahrig, speculoos owes its name to St. Nicholas, whose Latin epithet is speculator and means "the one who looks around, the guardian". Originally, it was given to children on 6 December. Another derivation recognises the Latin word speculum "mirror image" in the name and relates this to the models, which are traditionally often designed to depict small figures. Folklorist Gabi Grimm-Piecha said, "The term probably derives from speculator, translated overseer - which corresponds to the Latin name for bishop" and is an epithet of St. Nicholas in the Netherlands. "The biscuit used to be given to children on St. Nicholas Day, which was very special because of the expensive spices contained in the speculoos."

Oven temperature 200° C **Baking time** 10 - 12 minutes

Ingredients

500 g	Flour
1,5 TSP	Cinnamon
1 TSP	Ginger
¾ TSP	Cardamom
¼ TSP	Nutmeg
¼ TL	Mace
¼ TSP	White pepper
1/8 TSP.	Clove powder
1 TBSP.	Grated lemon peel
½ TSP	Baking Soda
½ TSP	Salt
180 g	Butter
200 g	brown sugar
90 ml	Water

Preparation

Beat the butter, sugar and water with a hand mixer for 10 minutes until fluffy. Then sprinkle in the spices, lemon zest and stir in.
Mix the flour with salt and baking soda, sift over the butter mixture and stir in thoroughly.
Knead the dough with your hands and form into a ball. Place this in a sealable container and leave to rest at room temperature for a few hours, preferably overnight.
Cover baking trays with baking paper. Roll out the dough thinly in small portions on a floured work surface. Cut out the dough with different designs.
Sprinkle a heap of flaked almonds flat on the baking tray, place a Spekulatius cut-out on top and press down lightly. Repeat with all the Spekulatius until the dough is used up. Then chill the trays for at least 15 minutes.
In the meantime, preheat the oven to 200 °C top/bottom heat.
Bake the trays one after the other in the preheated oven for 10 - 12 minutes on the middle shelf.
Store the cooled Spekulatius in a tin until ready to eat.

Vanilla Kipferl

Vanillekipferl originated in Vienna, Austria and are traditionally made at Christmas. They are very popular in Europe and are often found in Viennese coffee shops.

They are said to have been created in the shape of the Turkish crescent moon which celebrates the victory over the Turkish in 1683.

They are also widely known in Germany and are found in Switzerland, Hungary, Poland, Croatia, Czech Republic, Romania, and Slovakia as a part of the typical Christmas baking. Since in Germany the Advent is celebrated by several denominations of Christianity on the four Sundays preceding Christmas, many kinds of biscuits and sweets are consumed during this time and have become typical for wintertime. Unlike other pastries, this kind is difficult to bake.

When the batter has hardened it is very fragile. It takes skill to create the "kipferl" horse-shoe shape without breaking it!

Oven temperature 200° C **Baking time** about 8 minutes

Ingredients

450 g	Flour
375 g	Butter
150 g	Icing sugar
150 g	Almond(s), peeled and grated
150 g	Powdered sugar / icing sugar
6 pck.	Vanilla sugar

Preparation

Prepare a shortcrust pastry from flour, butter, 150 g icing sugar and almonds.

Place in the refrigerator for 1 hour.

Then roll the dough into thin sticks.

Cut into short pieces, form into rolls and bend into small croissants.

Place on a baking tray with baking paper and bake at 180° C fan oven for approx. 8 minutes until very light.

Remove from the baking sheet while still hot and immediately toss carefully in 150g confectioners' sugar and 4 packs of vanilla sugar, mixed well.

Christmas Stollen

There is one Christmas cake that I find particularly interesting, and that is the Dresden Christstollen. Only 112 stollen bakers from the city of Dresden are allowed to bake and sell original Dresden Christmas stollen.

The basic recipe for the stollen is fixed, but each of the 112 stollen bakers of the Schutzverband Dresdner Stollen e. V. has his or her own stollen secret, usually handed down for generations. Every year, the stollen of the 112 stollen bakers are tested to ensure identity, artisanship and taste. A committee of independent bakers and confectioners assesses the Stollen tests. Flavourings and preservatives are forbidden in genuine Dresden Christstollen. Every Stollen is made by hand. The longer the Christstollen lies, the more intense the bitter almond aroma becomes. This makes the stollen taste slightly like marzipan.

Dresden families bake their Christstollen on the 1st of Advent and cut it on the 24th of December. I find this tradition particularly beautiful.

Oven temperature *170˚ C* **Baking time** *about 35 - 45 minutes*

Ingredients for 2 stollen

400 g	Sultanas
200 g	Candied lemon peel
60 g	Candied orange peel
350 ml	Rum
250 ml	Milk
80 g	Fresh yeast
1	Pinch of sugar
1 kg	Flour
140 g	Sugar
1	Pinch of salt
3	Egg yolks
500 g	Butter
5 tr	Bitter almond oil
3 tbsp	Grated lemon zest
1/2 tsp	Ground cardamom
2	Vanilla pods
1	Pinch nutmeg
130 g	Chopped almonds, pecan nuts
	Baking paper
50 g	Butter
100 g	Icing sugar

Preparation

Finely chop the candied lemon peel and candied orange peel.
Mix together with the raisins in a bowl and pour over the orange juice. Leave to infuse for approx. 1 hour.
Drain well in a colander and set aside.
In a small saucepan, heat milk to lukewarm over moderate heat.
Crumble yeast and mix with approx. 1/8 litre lukewarm milk, 1 tablespoon sugar and a little flour.
Place flour in a large bowl. Make a well in the center.
Pour the pre-dough into the well and dust lightly with flour.
Sprinkle salt, sugar, and butter flakes over the top of the flour

Cover the bowl and let the pre-dough rise at room temperature for about 15 minutes.

Add remaining milk, egg yolk, bitter almond flavoring, lemon zest and cardamom.

Slit the vanilla pod, scrape out and add the pulp. Using the dough hook of a hand mixer (or your bare hands), mix all the ingredients together until it forms a smooth, silky dough and bubbles. Dust with flour and cover, then leave to rise for 10 minutes.

Remove dough from bowl, flatten on floured work surface with floured hands. Spread almonds, raisins, candied lemon peel and candied orange peel on top. Fold the four sides of the dough in towards the middle. Flatten the dough again, fold in again, and repeat, until the almonds and fruit are evenly distributed throughout the dough. Cover and leave to rest for 30 minutes.

Divide the dough in half and form an oblong roll from each half. Roll out thinly lengthwise in the middle with a floured rolling pin. Fold one side of the dough over the other and press down.

This is how the typical stollen shape comes about. Cover a baking tray with baking paper. Spread the two stollen on it and cover. Leave to rise for 30 minutes.

Bake the stollen in a preheated fan oven at 170 °C (convection oven) for 35-40 minutes. Then test them with a toothpick. If the dough still sticks to the toothpick, return the Stollen to the oven and bake for a few minutes longer. Be careful not to let them get too dark!

Melt butter in a saucepan, but do not brown. Brush the still warm stollen on all sides with it.

Sift thick powdered sugar over the top.

Let the stollen cool on a cooling rack and wrap tightly in aluminum foil to store. Store in a cool place.

Cinnamon Stars

Ingredients for 60 pieces

5	Egg white (cl. M)
415 g	Icing sugar
2	Packet vanilla sugar
4 TSP.	Cinnamon
660 g	Almonds (ground with brown skin)

Oven temperature 140° C **Baking time** about 25 minutes

Preparation

Beat the egg whites with a mixer until very stiff. Gradually sift in the icing sugar.

To coat the stars, remove 2 well heaped tbsp of meringue mixture. Combine vanilla sugar, cinnamon and half of the almonds and gently fold into the remaining meringue mixture with a dough scraper. Knead in enough of the rest of the almonds so that the dough barely sticks.

Cut open large freezer bag, sprinkle with a little ground almond and roll out dough to about 1 cm thick. Use a pastry cutter to cut out star shapes and place them on a baking tray lined with baking paper. Spread with the remaining meringue.

Place in the lower part of the oven for 25 minutes at 140 degrees top/bottom heat. Pull the cinnamon stars with the baking paper from the baking sheet and let them cool on a cooling rack.

Bread

&

Hearty Pastries

Bread History

The oldest remains of probably unleavened bread, 14,400 years old, were found in the Natufian settlement of Shubayqa 1 in north-eastern Jordan. These are charred bread remains made of wild cereals (einkorn), beach rushes and roots, which were excavated at ancient hearths. This proved that bread baking was developed at least about 4,000 years before the development of agriculture and cereal cultivation.

Then, about 10,000 years ago, humans began to systematically cultivate cereals for their own food. Originally, the grain was ground and eaten as porridge mixed with water. Later, the porridge was baked on hot stones or in ashes as flatbread. Baked flatbreads were probably already known to early nomadic peoples. Porridge cooked from wild grain and other ingredients was dried on hot stones and was thus durable and transportable.

Two inventions decisively changed the way bread was baked: One was the construction of baking ovens. Only flat loaves could be baked on the stones. A round loaf must be completely enclosed by the heat during baking so that it can bake evenly. The first ovens simply consisted of a pot that was inverted onto the hot stone (a method that scouts still like to practice around the campfire today).

The second important discovery that fundamentally changed bread baking was the effect of yeasts. If unbaked bread dough is left to stand, yeasts present in the air cause it to ferment - thin dough becomes a kind of fermented drink, thicker dough becomes yeast dough, which can be used to bake bread that is fluffier and tastier than that made from unfermented dough.

Since there are different yeast fungi that behave differently, these processes were initially very dependent on chance. Only in the course of time did man learn to control this by taking a small amount of the well-fermented dough before baking and adding it again to the next dough - the method of sourdough fermentation, which is still used today.

According to archaeological finds, leavened bread may have been
known more than 5,000 years ago, including in Egypt, where bread
was already produced on a large scale in bakeries at that time. In
ancient times, the Egyptians were also known as bread eaters. It
was they who first cultivated yeast and thus used the first baker's
yeast.
Baking ovens were further developed by the Egyptians, the first
ones were made of clay and resembled beehives. In them, a very
high heat could be achieved, which instantly transformed the
moisture present in the dough into steam. This greatly increased
the volume of the bread and delayed the formation of the crust.

Between 2860 and 1500 BC, 30 different types of bread (e.g. Chet
bread) were known in the land on the Nile. From Egypt, knowledge
of bread baking reached Europe via Greece and the Roman Empire.
The Romans built the first large mills and produced fine flour.
They invented a device for kneading dough: Stirring beaters were
moved in a trough via a mechanism by having an ox or a slave
walk around it.

North of the Alps, yeast doughs for making bread (either with
yeast from beer production, which had been known here since the
3rd millennium BC, or also from yeast mixtures such as sourdough)
were attested from 713 BC.

Bread was baked according to the basic Roman techniques, with
minor changes, in Europe until the 19th century. In several villages
there were communal ovens in which everyone could bake their
bread once a week.

A large Roman bakery was able to produce 36,000 kilograms of
bread per day 2000 years ago.
After the fall of the Roman Empire, white bread rose to the rank of
a festive and gentleman's dish.

It retained this position in Germany until after the Thirty Years'
War and in Russia until the beginning of the 20th century.
For the poorer classes, only dark bread was affordable.
In many countries, bread is used as the basis of soups and stews.

Farmhouse bread in the pot

Preparation time 20 min

Ingredients

400 g	Spelt flour 1050
100 g	Wholemeal spelt flour
1 ¾ tsp.	Salt
1 tbsp	Bread spice (see bread spice)
1/3 tsp.	Dry yeast
380 ml	Water
50 g	Butter liquid

Preparation

Mix both spelt flours, salt, sugar and yeast in a bowl. Add water and butter, mix well with a ladle, do not knead. Cover the dough and let it rise at room temperature for about 24 hours.

Transfer the dough to a well-floured work surface. Fold the dough in with the dough hook all the way round to the centre.
Turn the dough over and shape into a ball. Place the dough, seam side down, in a well-floured round or oval proofing basket, cover and leave to rise again for approx. 30 minutes.
Place the enamel pan with the lid in the bottom half of the oven.
Preheat the oven to 240 degrees and let the pot get really hot for about 15 minutes.
Remove the pot, flour the bottom of the pot well, turn the dough upside down out of the proofing basket into the hot roasting pot, put the lid on.

Bake: in the preheated oven with the lid on for the first 25 minutes and then without the lid for another 15 minutes.

Which pot is suitable for baking bread?

In principle, all ovenproof pots with tight-fitting lids are suitable for baking. Do not use pots with plastic parts or pots that are too cheap, as they can easily deform, or the coating or paint can peel off.

Cast-iron pots with lids and a volume of 4 liters are particularly recommended.
For this recipe I used a enamel pot, which is wonderfully suitable for this purpose.

Bread without kneading

Preparation time 15 min

Ingredients

600 g	Spelt flour 1050
2 tsp	Salt
1/2 tsp	Dried yeast
1 tbsp	Vinegar
400 ml	Water

Preparation

Mix the spelt flour, 2 tsp salt and ½ tsp dry yeast in a bowl. Add 400 ml water and 1 tbsp vinegar, mix with a spoon, do not knead. Cover and leave to rise for approx. 18 hours at room temperature until doubled.

Flatten the dough on a little flour, fold in half with floured hands, turn the dough, form into a ball, place on a floured cloth and dust with a little flour. Leave to rest for 30 minutes.

Bake: Place the casserole with the lid on a tray in the lower half of the oven. Preheat the oven to about 220 degrees. Take out the casserole, remove the lid, place the pastry in the hot casserole, cover and bake for about 30 minutes. Remove the lid and bake for about 20 minutes.

Remove the bread from the casserole dish, and place on a cooling rack.

Spelt- Rye bread with seeds

Preparation time 15 min

Ingredients for 1 loaf

300 g	Spelt flour
200g	Rye flour
55 g	Yeast fresh
450 ml	Water, lukewarm
2,5 Tbsp	Apple cider vinegar
2 TSP	Salt
70 g	Linseed coarsely ground
80 g	Sunflower seeds
1,5TL	Bread spice
	Grease for the mold

Preparation

Put the flour in a bowl and crumble in the yeast. Then add 450 ml lukewarm water and knead. Gradually knead the vinegar, salt, linseed and seeds into the dough.

Grease a loaf pan and pour in the batter.

Bake the bread for 60 minutes at 200°C with top and bottom heat. Remove the bread from the pan and continue baking for 8-10 minutes until it is lightly browned on the bottom. When it sounds hollow by tapping on the underside, it is ready.

Crispbread with seeds

Ingredients

250 g	Spelt flour
250 g	Small spelt flakes
50 g	Grated almonds
200 g	Mixed nuts (3 varieties)
3 Tbsp	Olive oil or ghee
400 ml	Cold water
2 TSP.	Sea salt

Nut mixture for example

125 g	Roasted sesame
25 g	Linseed
50 g	Sunflower seeds

Preparation

Place flour and flakes in a mixing bowl with the remaining dry ingredients and mix well. Add oil and water and mix until a tough dough is formed.

Divide the dough in half and spread or roll out each half evenly and thinly on two baking sheets lined with baking paper.

Tip: Rinse rolling pin with cold water in between or place a plastic foil the size of the baking tray on the dough. This makes the roll-out easier.

Finish with a spatula or knife to cut the dough into large slices of bread.

Preheat the oven to 200 ° C. Preheat the oven (convection) and the baking tray to 200 ° C.

Bake for about 7 minutes.

Then switch the temperature back to 170 ° C and bake for 20-25 minutes.

Immediately remove the crispbread from the tray and let it cool. Then store the finished crispbread in a bread box.

Pesto Flower

Ingredients for 1 flower

500 g	Spelt flour
250 ml	Water, lukewarm
50 g	Yeast
1 TSP	Sugar
2 TSP	Salt
50 ml	Oil
200 g	Pesto

Preparation

Crumble the yeast and dissolve it in some of the lukewarm water.
Knead flour, remaining water, sugar, yeast water, salt and oil to a
yeast dough and let it rest covered for half an hour.
Then divide the yeast dough into 3 equal parts. Roll out the dough
pieces in a round shape, for this it is best to place a spring-form
base or a round cake board underneath to get a nice round shape.

Spread first round of dough with a generous amount of pesto and
place the next layer of dough on top. Spread again with pesto. If
you like, you can use a different coloured pesto. Place the last layer
of dough on top.

Cut the dough into 16 pieces - first quarter the circle and then
quarter the quarters again.

In the middle must be left free circle, so that the pieces are not
loose, but connected to the center.

Take 2 parts in your hand and turn them outwards twice.
Proceed in the same way with all further parts.

Finally, you can connect the individual ends together to create
beautiful leaves.

Preheat oven to 190° - 200° top/bottom heat and bake for approx. 20
- 25 minutes.

Sourdough baguette

Ingredients for 3 baguettes

500 g	Flour (wheat flour type 550)
100 g	Sourdough (wheat sourdough), liquid
5 g	Yeast
10 g	Salt
270 g	Water

Preparation

Dissolve the yeast in 100 ml of the weighed-out amount of water.
Add all other ingredients and knead well (works especially well in
a food processor). Let the dough rise at room temperature for about
20 minutes.

Divide the dough into three pieces of equal weight. Shape the pieces
into rounds and let them rise on a floured work surface, covered
with a damp cloth, for 40 minutes.

Shape the balls into baguettes with pointed ends and place on a
baking tray lined with baking paper. Leave as much space as
possible, as the baguettes will rise a lot!

Now let them rise for another 1 1/2 hours.

Preheat the oven to about 220°C.

Dust the baguettes lightly with flour and make several diagonal
cuts. Pour a cup of water on the bottom of the oven (be careful,
danger of burning!) and put the baking tray into the oven. Bake for
about 20 - 30 minutes, until the baguettes have a golden-brown
crust.

Sourdough

The basis for many different breads is the sourdough. But some people often shy away from the preparation of this base. Why, actually? Making sourdough yourself is very simple. All you need is water and flour and a little time. Not working time, but time for the dough to become sour. How to do this, you can read here.

Ingredients for sourdough

100 g   Rye flour
100 ml   Tap water

Prepare sourdough

Please keep in mind that sourdough needs about 5 days until you can use it. Only then is the dough so sour that you can call it sourdough.
So quickly mixing a dough and then using it as a base for sour bread does not work. But if you have a base for sourdough, after 5 days you can keep feeding that on and so you have sourdough at home all the time. So, here we go...

Make sourdough 1. day

On the first day, put 100g of flour and 100 ml of water in a container and stir the mixture well. Now the dough must rest for at least 24, but better 48 hours, covered and at room temperature (21-24 degrees).

Making sourdough day 2-5

Now that the dough has rested for at least 24 hours, add 50g of flour and 50ml of water each day. This process is called "feeding". Do this for a total of 4 days.

So on day 5 the sourdough has been "fed" 100g of rye flour from the first day and 4 times 50g from the other days. So in total you need 300g of flour. And in addition, the dough has received the same amount of water, in this case also 300ml of water.
On the 5th day, let the sourdough rest for another 24 hours until you are ready to use it on the 6th day.
Use sourdough again and again.

Congratulations!

You have now made sourdough for 1 loaf of bread. From the total mixture (600g) you can now use ½ kilo for your bread.
Then feed again 200g flour and 200ml water. Let the dough rest again for 24 hours.
You can then put it in the fridge where it will keep for about 3-4 days, or freeze it, this will make the sourdough last for months!

So, you always have fresh sourdough for your favorite bread at home.

Bread spice

Ingredients

2 Tbsp	Fennel seeds
2 Tbsp	Caraway
2 Tbsp	Anise
1 Tbsp	Coriander

Preparation

Finely grind all ingredients in a moulinette or similar device. Store in a tightly closed jar

For 500g flour take about 2 tablespoons of spice.

For white bread at most a pinch. That is a matter of taste.

If you make small quantities, you have a guarantee that the spice won't lose its flavor.